KV-577-773

Finchley Church End
Library
020 8359 3800

Please return/renew this item by the
last date shown to avoid a charge.
Books may also be renewed by phone
and Internet. May not be renewed if
required by another reader.

www.libraries.barnet.gov.uk

BARNET
LONDON BOROUGH

Written by June Eison

Illustrated by Jennifer Jamieson

HODDER

Hachette UK's policy is to use papers that are natural, renewable and recyclable products and made from wood grown in well-managed forests and other controlled sources. The logging and manufacturing processes are expected to conform to the environmental regulations of the country of origin.

ISBN: 9781398377066

Text © Jane Elson
Illustrations, design and layout © Hodder and Stoughton Ltd
First published in 2023 by Hodder & Stoughton Limited (for its Hodder Education imprint, part of the Hodder Education Group),
An Hachette UK Company
Carmelite House, 50 Victoria Embankment, London EC4Y 0DZ

www.hoddereducation.com

Impression number 10 9 8 7 6 5 4 3 2 1
Year 2027 2026 2025 2024 2023

Author: Jane Elson
Series Editor: Catherine Coe
Commissioning Editor: Hamish Baxter
Illustrator: Jennifer Jamieson/The Plum Agency
Educational Reviewer: Pauline Allen
Design and page layouts: Rocket Design (East Anglia) Ltd
Editor: Amy Tyrer

With thanks to the schools that took part in the development of *Reading Planet KS2*, including: Ancaster CE Primary School, Ancaster; Downsway Primary School, Reading; Ferry Lane Primary School, London; Foxborough Primary School, Slough; Griffin Park Primary School, Blackburn; St Barnabas CE First & Middle School, Pershore; Tranmoor Primary School, Doncaster; and Wilton CE Primary School, Wilton.

The publishers would like to thank the following for permission to reproduce copyright material. Wooden plank © dule964/AdobeStock; splat © grumpybox/AdobeStock; Blackboard & frame © thanapun/frender/AdobeStock.

A catalogue record for this title is available from the British Library.

Printed in the UK.

Orders: Please contact Hachette UK Distribution, Hely Hutchinson Centre, Milton Road, Didcot, Oxfordshire, OX11 7HH. Telephone: +44 (0)1235 400555. Email: primary@hachette.co.uk.

Contents

Chapter 1

I, Colindale Digby, dream of winning the Golden Dance Cup of Excellence. It's awarded by Madame Bertha's Ballet and Tap Academy, where I have ballet lessons. I dream every night that I am kissing the cup and holding it in the air as the crowds cheer.

I dream that my name is added to all the other names engraved on the cup. But there is one year – 1940 – that doesn't have a name. There is just a gap where the name should be. I always wonder who won it that year. Why isn't their name engraved on the cup?

I'm always first into the studio so I can warm up, but today there is a boy standing by the cabinet, staring at the Golden Dance Cup of Excellence.

"Hello," I say.

He spins round. I have not seen him before in our village. It would be brilliant to have another boy in my ballet class as I am the only one.

"Hi, I'm Digby," I say. "I'll take you to see Madame Bertha. What's your name?"

"I've changed my mind," he mumbles and runs out of the studio.

"You will enjoy ballet," I call after him, but he's gone. I shrug and start to warm up as the rest of my class pour into the room, chattering.

We have to dance in front of the whole village of Ashton in three days' time, and the winner of the cup shall be decided. I so want it to be me.

For the past six years, it has been won by the mayor's daughter, Chrystal Kelly, who is very bendy and does a lot of tap dancing.

A breeze comes through the window of the dance studio, which is open at the top. I can hear a drill in the distance. A water pipe burst on the only road out of the village last week. All the grown-ups do is groan on about how you can't get in and out of our village at the moment.

I wave as I dance past the window. My best friend in the whole world, Marvel, is dancing outside. She's swirling around in her purple cloak, with the autumn leaves fluttering around her as they fall from the trees. She won't come inside. She doesn't like being too close to people, and she says the noise hurts her ears. She always wears the purple magician's cloak because she is obsessed by the magician, illusionist and great escape artist Houdini.

I see her dance off round the building towards the village square. She is always in her own world.

A flash of sunlight shines in my eyes, and I wobble. There's a crash as the window cleaner bangs his bucket down to mop his brow. The old window cleaner was Henry, who always used to chat and laugh with us. But he fell off his ladder and broke his leg.

I don't know this new one. He marches off with his ladder round the corner.

A bird squawks from the tree outside. I look upwards as the bird flies off and see a face vanish into the leafy branches of the tree. It's the boy who ran out of the dance studio. What's he doing up in a tree? Maybe he wants to spy on our ballet class to see if he'd enjoy it. I hope he likes it and joins.

"Colindale Digby, concentrate, please," shouts Madame Bertha, clapping her hands.

Today we are doing *pas de chat*, which is French for 'step of the cat'. It's my favourite dance step.

Tap, tap, tap. Madame Bertha is banging her cane on the dance floor and glaring at me, and I realise that everyone has gone to the left and I have gone to the right. I always get left and right confused.

"Digby, on your own, please," Madame Bertha says, clapping her hands.

Everyone clears to the sides to watch me. So I do my very best *pas de chat* away from the window, towards the opposite wall.

Then I do the *pas de chat* in the other direction, towards the window and the cabinet in the corner where the Golden Dance Cup of Excellence is displayed. I'm hoping and imagining that in three days' time it will be mine.

But there is a clatter. It's Marmaduke, our school caretaker's ginger cat. His face is flat against the window, staring in at us. He's trying to come into our ballet studio. But he has this smug expression on his face, as if it is only he who can dance a *pas de chat*.

I can't help it but Marmaduke makes me burst out laughing. Then the sunlight shines in my eyes again, and I somehow wobble so badly that I trip over my own feet and fall flat on my face. I can't get up as I am laughing so hard. All the class crowd round me, laughing too. Madame Bertha is banging her cane on the floor, shouting, "This is disgraceful behaviour," but that only makes us laugh louder. Chrystal holds her hand out and I grab hold of it to pull myself up. Marmaduke has vanished from the windowsill.

"Quiet, class. Attention, please," says Madame Bertha, banging her cane hard on the floor. "We have only three days before the winner of the Golden Dance Cup of Excellence is decided."

I know there's no time to lose.

Gradually, everyone swallows their giggles. I take a deep breath to try to stop laughing. My breath turns to a gasp! The Golden Dance Cup of Excellence has gone. The cabinet is empty!

Madame Bertha has sent us all home while she calls the police. Marvel comes dancing towards me from the village square. I run to meet her, holding on to the deerstalker hat our friend Bee gave me so it doesn't fall off.

"The cup has been stolen from under our noses," I say. "This is a mystery for the Digby and Marvel Detective Agency."

"Yes, we must solve the mystery of the missing Golden Dance Cup of Excellence," says Marvel, and she drags me by my hand through the village. We go all the way to the garden shed in the allotments of the Rise and Shine Happy Care Home for Older People, which is the Digby and Marvel Detective Agency headquarters.

"We must use our superpowers of alternative thinking," says Marvel. "We shall use them to find out who has stolen the Golden Dance Cup of Excellence."

"But we only have three days to get it back," I say.

Chapter 2

I love our Digby and Marvel Detective Agency headquarters. I look round at the table in the corner with plant pots on it. There's an old pair of gardening gloves lying next to them, and a wheelbarrow in the corner with a spade and trowel and gardening fork inside. On the floor lies an old sack.

Most importantly, on the wall is the map of our village, and next to it is an old chalkboard.

"The Golden Dance Cup of Excellence must still be in the village somewhere since nobody can get out because of the burst water pipe," I say.

"Good thinking, Digby," says Marvel.

"We should make a list of suspects," I say. I get a bit of chalk from out of my pocket and write.

SUSPEKTS
Windo Cleener

"Excellent detective skills," says Marvel. "This new window cleaner is a stranger. Don't you think we should add the boy who you saw in the studio and up the tree to the suspect list?"

"No," I say, "it can't be him because he ran out of Madame Bertha's and the cup was still there. When I fell over and we were all laughing, it was a distraction," I say.

"That is what the great Houdini did," says Marvel. "He distracted his audience while he worked his magic. The Golden Dance Cup of Excellence vanished when you were on the floor laughing. Everyone was looking at you, not the cabinet."

"We need to go back to the scene of the crime to look for clues," I say.

"There is no time to waste," says Marvel. "We must use our brain powers to solve this mystery."

"What about Gloria?" I say. "Won't she wonder where you are?"

"She will think I am helping and talking to the old people at the Rise and Shine Happy Care Home for Older People."

Marvel loves to help the old people and talk to them about her favourite subject, Houdini. She likes talking to them better than the kids at Ashton Junior School.

"What about your mum and dad?" says Marvel.

I text Mum.

MUM

With Marvel helpin old peeple

"But that is a lie," says Marvel.

"It's not a lie," I say, "because if we find the Golden Dance Cup of Excellence the old people will be happy. The whole of Ashton will be happy."

Marvel is chewing her lip and shaking her hands. She does this sometimes when her brain overloads.

"I suppose so," she says.

14

"Come on," I say. "We have no time to lose."

We run out of our headquarters, up Duck Street.

Chrystal is walking on her hands in her garden, her gold curls trailing on the grass, her hands covered in mud. She doesn't see us as we run past.

"Chrystal might have taken it and buried the cup in the garden," says Marvel. "She can see your ballet is brilliant and she's scared of not winning again this year."

"We'll add her to our suspect list," I say.

We reach Madame Bertha's Ballet and Tap Academy. We duck behind a bush just as our village police officer, PC Rob, walks out of the entrance and climbs into a police car. Next to him is a female police officer. "That's PC Laura," whispers Marvel. "She came to Ashton Juniors when I was six years, two months and two days old to talk to us about Stranger Danger."

"You remember everything," I say.

Marvel taps her head twice and grabs my arm.

"Now," she says, and we jump up and run round the back of Madame Bertha's, until we're in the garden, looking through the window at the ballet studio and the empty cabinet.

"I think the thief must have got in through the back," says Marvel.

"But surely we would've seen a stranger in our ballet studio," I say.

"That is how magicians like Houdini work," says Marvel. "They make the audience look in one direction while they do the trick in the other."

"Look," I say, reaching up to a branch. A tiny thread of light brown wool is dangling from a twig.

"Here is another one," says Marvel. She points to a thread of wool caught in the bark of the tree.

I take my trainer and sock off.

"It smells of tuna," says Marvel.

"What, my smelly sock?" I say, laughing.

"No, the wool. I have a very fine-tuned sense of smell," says Marvel.

I wrap the two bits of wool in my sock, so they don't get lost, and put it in my pocket.

"The Digby and Marvel Detective Agency now have their very first clues," I say.

"It is eating time," says Marvel. "We must go home."

As we walk through the village square, some rubbish blows out of the bin and clatters to the floor.

We run to pick it up. It's an old pizza box, some squashed chips and an empty can of tuna.

"The wool smelled of fish," says Marvel. "The empty tuna can might be a clue, Digby."

"You're right, Marvel," I say and wrap the can in my sock with the bits of wool.

We cut through the woods towards Old Alice's red
wagon. She's feeding the feral cats.

There are ginger, black, tabby, grey and white cats
everywhere, scrapping over food, drinking from
puddles, snoozing in branches, scampering around,
mewing, purring and hissing. Marmaduke has
wandered into the middle of them and is having a
stand-off with a huge black cat. Marmaduke should
not be here – it's not his territory.

There's the sound of clanking metal. Through the
woods runs the boy who was in Madame Bertha's
studio, with cans tied to a long string of brown wool
trailing behind him. Several of the cats are chasing
him, pouncing on the cans and playing.

"Hello," I call, but he's gone.

Chapter 3

Ballet class at Madame Bertha's the next day just isn't the same without the Golden Dance Cup of Excellence shining at me from the cabinet, encouraging me to point my toes harder and jump higher. All I can think about is that the Digby and Marvel Detective Agency only have two days to find the cup.

Madame Bertha's not happy with any of us, especially me.

"Colindale Digby," she says, banging her cane on the floor. "That is not a *pas de chat*, the step of the cat – that is more like the step of the hamster."

The whole class are giggling, and Lucy and Chrystal start whispering in the corner.

"QUIET!" shouts Madame Bertha, banging her cane harder. "You should be dancing with your feet not your mouths."

As we dance round in a circle, I catch a glimpse of purple behind a bush.

It's Marvel – she's not dancing outside today but hiding, waiting for the class to finish.

Finally, the girls curtsey and I bow, as we do at the end of every class. I get changed slowly. I need to be the last one in the dance studio so we can carry on our investigation.

I drag the massive lost property box out of the cupboard to give me even more of an excuse to be last out. I find three pairs of ballet tights and four odd ballet shoes in the box that are all mine.

I wait until all the children, and the grown-ups who are collecting them, have gone, and I hear the tap of Madame Bertha's cane as she climbs the stairs to her flat, above the academy. Then I know it is safe for Marvel to come into the dance studio. I beckon her in.

She jumps up from behind the bush, scurries to the door and creeps into the dance studio.

Marvel stumbles, and out from the bottom of her purple cloak appears Marmaduke.

"He keeps winding through my legs, tripping me up," says Marvel.

"Marmaduke!" I say, bending down to stroke the cat, but he leaps on Marvel's shoulder and stays there. "He's not usually this friendly," I say.

Marmaduke gives me an unloving look. "We need to examine the scene of the crime," I say, and we run over to the empty cabinet and open it. Marmaduke leaps off Marvel's shoulder and into the cabinet and starts licking the wood.

Marvel leans forwards and sniffs.

"Tuna," she says.

Tap, tap, tap. It's Madame Bertha! She's coming down the stairs.

"Quick, hide," I whisper. We run over to the lost property box and jump in, crouching there, huddled together.

Marvel is shaking, and I know that she must hate being in here among the old smelly tights, leotards and old ballet shoes. I put my arm round her and hug my friend tight.

I hold my breath. Supposing Madame Bertha looks in the box and we are caught? I hear the *tap, tap, tap* as she goes over to the cabinet.

"Marmaduke, come out of there, you silly cat," she says. I hear a yowl and a thud as Marmaduke lands on the floor. Then the sound of *tap, tap, tap* and purring as Marmaduke follows Madame Bertha out of the dance studio.

I am tangled in tights and Marvel has a ballet shoe on her head.

"Let's get out of here," I say.

And we run as fast as we can back to the Digby and Marvel Detective Agency headquarters.

Chapter 4

We lay out our clues. An empty tuna can and two threads of brown wool. I update our suspect list.

SUSPEKTS

Windo Cleener
Kristel

"It is not a lot to go on," says Marvel.

"We've got to solve the mystery by tomorrow," I say. "We just have to."

"The burst pipe means that the thief would not have been able to drive off with the cup," says Marvel.

"It must be somewhere in the village," I say, staring at our map. "But where?"

My tummy rumbles and the tinkle of the piano reaches my ears. It's Matilda from the Rise and Shine. She loves to play musicals. She's playing a song about Macavity the Mystery Cat from the musical *Cats*. I start humming along a line to myself: "For he's the master criminal who can defy the Law."

"It's time to have tea and cake with the old people," I say.

There are a lot of relatives visiting the old people today in the Rise and Shine. Sid, Millie, Linford and Mabel are all enjoying themselves as they sing along to the piano, chat to relatives and drink tea.

I cut two slices of chocolate cake and hand one to Marvel.

There in the corner, sitting on a huge armchair and reading a magazine, is the boy I last saw running through the woods, chased by cats.

I nudge Marvel. "It's him," she whispers.

The boy looks up and sees us staring at him. Looking startled, he drops the magazine on the floor, and a receipt flutters out of it.

I run to pick them up and see this receipt is for a cat laser-light toy.

"Meet my grandson, Oliver," calls Matilda from behind the piano as I pass the magazine and receipt to him.

"Hi, Oliver," I say.

"Hello, Oliver," says Marvel. "I am very pleased to meet you." But he ignores us and carries on reading.

Marvel flaps her hands and starts reciting all the names of the people who have ever won the Golden Dance Cup of Excellence.

She has an amazing memory, and she does this to comfort herself when there are too many strangers around. I'm not properly listening because for the last six years it's been Chrystal Kelly – Chrystal Kelly – Chrystal Kelly – on and on. But then Marvel starts twirling back through the years – Alice Morden, Claire Bradford – back and back she goes. Until she gets to 1940, the year with no name.

We both say together, "Who was the year of the gap?"

"It was me," says Matilda, and she stops playing the piano. "I was the year of the gap."

Everybody stops talking.

"It was the war," Matilda says, "and I loved to dance. We had a concert in Ashton and my ballet dance won the Golden Dance Cup of Excellence. I reached out to hold it in my hands, but the sirens wailed and we had to run to the shelters. The year 1940 was engraved on the cup ready for the winner's name. But I never did get to have my name engraved because the next day we moved up to Scotland to stay with my Aunty Bess for the rest of the war. When we moved back to the village, the dance school was closed.

When Madame Bertha's grandmother reopened the school after the war, everything had changed. I thought it was too late to say it should be my name by 1940. I never even got to hold the golden cup in my hands."

My thoughts are dancing round my brain. Imagine winning and not even getting your name engraved on the cup. I want my name engraved on the cup so badly it actually hurts.

"We've got to find the Golden Dance Cup of Excellence," I say.

"It has got to be somewhere in the village," says Marvel.

I swallow my last mouthful of chocolate cake and put the plate back on the tea trolley. I turn round and see an empty armchair.

Oliver has gone.

Chapter 5

"Where's my grandson?" says Matilda. "Where has Oliver got to now? He's always disappearing, that boy."

"We'll go and find him," I say to Matilda. "And search for the Golden Dance Cup of Excellence at the same time," I whisper to Marvel. "Come on."

So we walk through Ashton, with the houses on one side and the old people's flowers and vegetables on the other.

I am keeping a lookout for places where the thief might have hidden the Golden Dance Cup of Excellence.

"Oliver, Oliver, where are you?" we call, but there is no reply.

"We should go to our headquarters," I say. "The shed is the obvious place to hide." We run over to our shed and open the door.

I gasp. The strands of wool and the empty tuna can have gone! Our clues have been taken!

The heaviness of despair fills me from top to toe. "Whoever has been in our headquarters is on to us," I say. "We're never going to find the Golden Dance Cup of Excellence in time for tomorrow."

"Look, someone has been sitting on the sack on the floor," says Marvel. "There is a small dent in it."

"You're a brilliant detective," I say. "You notice every little detail."

"So are you," says Marvel. "You have the gift of alternative thinking."

But my brain feels like a scrambled ball of string. I don't feel I can do any thinking at all.

We wander out of the door of our headquarters, through the old people's flowers and back on to the road.

We reach the crooked bridge and go over the river, calling, "Oliver," all the time. We pass the Town Hall and swimming pool and reach Madame Bertha's Ballet and Tap Academy.

When I see the tree that Oliver was hiding in, the knots in my brain tug at each other.

"We have the window cleaner and Chrystal as suspects," I say. "But supposing Oliver did have something to do with the missing Golden Dance Cup of Excellence? I just can't work out how! Maybe it was Marmaduke?" I say, laughing.

I start humming the lyrics of the song that Matilda was playing – about Macavity the Mystery Cat 'who can defy the Law'.

"That's it!" Suddenly, I know who stole the cup. "IT WAS MARMADUKE!" I shout.

"How can it be?" says Marvel. "He is a cat."

My tangled brain starts to unravel. "What if it was an actual cat burglar?"

"There was the smell of tuna," says Marvel, "on the threads of wool and inside the cabinet."

"Yes," I say. "Oliver lured Marmaduke in there by planting the fish smell, and he must have been attaching the wool to the cup when I walked in. Yes, and there was the receipt for the cat laser toy in Oliver's magazine. That wasn't sunlight that made me fall over – it was Oliver shining the laser light."

"So, from up in the tree," says Marvel, "Oliver would have tight hold of one end of the brown wool. Oliver encouraged Marmaduke in through the window, using the cat laser toy. Marmaduke would have chased the light into the studio, smelled the tuna and run over to the cabinet. Then, seeing the wool attached to the cup, it would have looked like a giant cat toy to him. He would have batted it with his paw on to the ground."

"Yes," I say.

"Then Oliver would have pulled his end of the thread, and the cup would have dragged along the floor with Marmaduke chasing it. He would have pulled it out of the window and made his escape. The threads we found were where the wool caught on twigs."

"It is a genius plan," says Marvel. "If Oliver had walked out of Madame Bertha's with the cup, he would have been seen and arrested as a thief, but no one is going to arrest Marmaduke, are they? He is a cat. And, what's more, I think Oliver shone the laser in your eyes deliberately to make you fall and cause a distraction. The great Houdini could not have done better."

And we both look at each other and say at exactly the same time:

"We have to find Oliver to make him tell us where the Golden Dance Cup of Excellence is hidden."

Chapter 6

"I think Oliver might have made for the woods," says Marvel.

"Yes, it's the best hiding place," I say. "And we saw him there yesterday, playing with the cats."

We run through the village square until we reach the trees. It's starting to get dark. An owl hoots. The trees' dark twisty branches snatch at our clothes.

"Ah! I'm stuck," says Marvel. Her purple cloak is caught in some twigs. I run to untangle my friend and on we go, through the dark, until we see the silhouette of Old Alice's wagon in the moonlight. She is sitting on the steps. All around her are mewling, sleeping, hissing, purring, playing cats, but there's no sign of the cup.

"Look," says Marvel, and she pulls a long strand of brown wool caught on some twigs on the floor. The cup has been here.

"Have you seen a boy, Old Alice?" I call.

"He went that way," she says and points towards the river.

We run through the dark.

"Look, footprints, in the mud," I call.

"Well spotted, Digby," says Marvel, and we follow them. Soon, we reach a big oak tree by the river, where Oliver is sitting, huddled in a ball. Next to him, on the ground, are our clues. The two strands of wool and the tuna can.

We creep up to him, so he doesn't hear us and run.

"Oliver," says Marvel. "Please, what have you done with the Golden Dance Cup of Excellence?"

He looks up, and his face crumples as he points to the river.

There, on top of a bed of pebbles in the river, lies the golden cup.

"Why did you steal it?" I asked. "We know you used Marmaduke as a cat burglar."

"I was only planning to borrow it, so that my gran would be able to hold it," says Oliver. "I knew it's her dearest wish, only she doesn't like to make a fuss."

"And you planted the wool and the tuna smell, and used Marmaduke to help bat it out with his paw," says Marvel.

Oliver nods. "When I dragged it out of the window, I ran till I reached the woods, but the feral cats licked it and chased it and batted it with their paws until it fell in the river. Now I can't get it back. I keep trying to reach it, but I can't."

"Hello," comes a call through the trees. Torchlight shines through the branches. It's Matilda, Sid, Millie, Linford and Mabel from the Rise and Shine.

"We're over here," I shout, "and we've got Oliver."

A way to solve the problem is forming in my brain.

Five minutes later, we've formed a chain, with me at the end. Every link in the chain is holding hands tight with each other so that I don't fall in. Marvel is the next link in the chain to me.

"You can do this," she says.

I reach into the cold river and I grab hold of the Golden Dance Cup of Excellence.

"Hello, hello," echoes through the trees. More torchlight comes through the woods. It's PC Rob and PC Laura.

"You are too late," calls out Marvel. "The Digby and Marvel Detective Agency have solved the mystery of the missing Golden Dance Cup of Excellence."

It's the day of the dance contest, and I dance and point my feet like I never have before. When I do my *pas de chat*, not Marmaduke nor any of the feral cats could have done it better.

Everyone has danced. It is time for the winner to be announced. I hold my breath as the mayor announces, "The winner is Colindale Digby!"

I have never felt happier in my life, but I know what I must do.

"Congratulations," says Chrystal, which is kind of her. I know how disappointed she must be not to win the cup for the seventh year.

Marvel and Gloria, and my mum and dad, are all applauding from the front row. The old people in the second row wave their sticks in the air.

"Ladies and gentleman," I shout, and everyone falls silent. "I am not the only winner today. A long time ago, Matilda won the Golden Dance Cup of Excellence, but she did not get to hold it because of the war. Matilda, will you join me on the stage, please?"

Matilda is helped on to the stage, and we hold the cup high in the air together. Tears of happiness are trickling down her cheeks as everyone stands up and cheers.

The next day, we have a new pupil at Madame Bertha's – Oliver Laurie. I smile at him and show him where to change before we take our place at the barre. It will be nice not being the only boy.

The Golden Dance Cup of Excellence is back in the cabinet at Madame Bertha's, and there is no longer a gap – but the name 'Matilda Laurie' is engraved clearly for all to see.

And at the top of the names is Colindale Digby.

The End

Now answer the questions ...

1 What does Digby dream of winning?

2 What is '*pas de chat*' French for?

3 What does 'alternative' mean in the line, "We must use our superpowers of alternative thinking" on page 11?

4 Why isn't Madame Bertha happy with anyone in the ballet class at the beginning of Chapter 3?

5 What happens when Digby and Marvel go to have tea and cake at the Rise and Shine Happy Care Home for Older People?

6 Look at the line 'But my brain feels like a scrambled ball of string' on page 29. Why might the author have used these particular words to describe how Digby was feeling?

7 What did you think would happen when they found Oliver in the woods?

8 How do you feel about what Oliver did? Do you think he was right to take the cup to make his gran feel better?